CYRANO DE BERGERAC

Edmond Rostand

EDITORIAL DIRECTOR Maxwell Krohn
EDITORIAL DIRECTOR Justin Kestler
MANAGING EDITOR Ben Florman

SERIES EDITORS Boomie Aglietti, Justin Kestler
PRODUCTION Christian Lorentzen

WRITERS Brian Phillips, James Sitar
EDITORS Benjamin Morgan, Jesse Hawkes

Copyright © 2002 by SparkNotes LLC

All rights reserved. No part of this book may be used or reproduced in any manner whatsoever without the written permission of the Publisher.

SPARKNOTES is a registered trademark of SparkNotes LLC.

This edition published by Spark Publishing

Spark Publishing
A Division of SparkNotes LLC
120 Fifth Avenue, 8th Floor
New York, NY 10011

Any book purchased without a cover is stolen property, reported as "unsold and destroyed" to the Publisher, who receives no payment for such "stripped books."

05 SN 9 8 7 6 5 4 3 2

Please send all comments and questions or report errors to
feedback@sparknotes.com.

Library of Congress information available upon request

Printed and bound in the United States

RRD-C

ISBN 1-58663-507-7

INTRODUCTION: STOPPING TO BUY SPARKNOTES ON A SNOWY EVENING

Whose words these are you *think* you know.
Your paper's due tomorrow, though;
We're glad to see you stopping here
To get some help before you go.

Lost your course? You'll find it here.
Face tests and essays without fear.
Between the words, good grades at stake:
Get great results throughout the year.

Once school bells caused your heart to quake
As teachers circled each mistake.
Use SparkNotes and no longer weep,
Ace every single test you take.

Yes, books are lovely, dark, and deep,
But only what you grasp you keep,
With hours to go before you sleep,
With hours to go before you sleep.

CONTENTS

NOTE: This SparkNote refers to the Signet classic edition of *Cyrano de Bergerac: Heroic Comedy in Five Acts,* translated by Lowell Bair. The names of places and smaller characters may differ from translation to translation.

Context

Edmond Rostand was born in Marseilles, France, in 1868. His father, a part-time poet, pushed Edmond toward a law career, but as a college student in Paris, he instead fell in love with French literature and theater. He eventually did earn a law degree, but he focused primarily on succeeding in his first love, the theater. His early career featured a string of accomplishments: his first play, *Le Gant Rouge,* was produced when he was only twenty years old, and his next two plays followed shortly. Each new play proved more successful than the previous one, and Rostand's name began to lure prominent actors and actresses to star in his productions.

In 1897, Rostand enjoyed his greatest triumph with the production of his sensationally popular *Cyrano de Bergerac.* With the famous Benoit Constant Coquelin (to whom the play is dedicated) performing the lead role, the play was a tremendous success. Late nineteenth-century theater had been dominated by grim, realistic stories and unsentimental characters. But in *Cyrano de Bergerac,* Rostand departed from the realist tradition to present an unabashed historical romance, set in the 1640s and featuring a swashbuckling hero. Audiences loved the play's passionate love story, comedy, fast-paced action, and tragic ending. Above all, they responded powerfully to the larger-than-life character of Cyrano, the genius hero with a ridiculously long nose. After *Cyrano de Bergerac,* Rostand's career began to slowly decline, and he never again enjoyed the kind of success he had achieved with *Cyrano.* He died in 1918, but his most popular creation continues to live on in hundreds of productions. Most recently, the play spawned a pair of popular films: the French *Cyrano de Bergerac,* starring Gerard Depardieu, and the modernized American adaptation, *Roxanne,* starring Steve Martin.

While Rostand wrote more than a century ago, the play evokes an even older era: France during the age of Louis XIII. In the nineteenth century, it was popular to romantically recall this seventeenth-century era as France's golden age—a time when men were musketeers, women were beautiful heiresses, and the wit flashed as brightly as the swordplay. In fact, Alexandre Dumas had published his famous sentimental romance, *The Three Musketeers,* a full half-century before *Cyrano* took to the stage. *Cyrano* parodied, paid homage to, and proved itself a blatant copy of Dumas's popular novel. Nineteenth-century audiences viewed Cyrano's honesty, courage, wit, passion, and extraordinary willpower as the embodiment of this lost golden age. The play sounded a clarion call to remind France of what it believed it had lost.

The real Cyrano de Bergerac is a novelist and playwright who lived from 1619 to 1655, around the same time as the fictional Cyrano. The real Cyrano probably inspired the idea for Rostand's protagonist, but the play's events, as well as its other characters, are solely the product of Rostand's imagination.

PLOT OVERVIEW

I N PARIS, IN THE YEAR 1640, a brilliant poet and swordsman named Cyrano de Bergerac finds himself deeply in love with his beautiful, intellectual cousin Roxane. Despite Cyrano's brilliance and charisma, a shockingly large nose afflicts his appearance, and he considers himself too ugly even to risk telling Roxane his feelings. One night, Cyrano goes to the playhouse at the Hotel de Bourgogne to make trouble: he has forbidden the actor Montfleury to take the stage for one month, but Montfleury plans to perform in the night's production of *La Clorise,* with Roxane in the audience. Also in the audience is a young, handsome nobleman named Christian, who confides in his friend Ligniere that he loves Roxane.

When Montfleury takes the stage, Cyrano bullies him off it. A group of aristocrats tries to send Cyrano away, but he challenges them all to a duel. He fights Valvert, a Vicomte whom the Comte de Guiche has selected as a husband for Roxane. As he fights, Cyrano improvises a poem about the duel. Then, upon speaking his last line, Cyrano thrusts his sword home. His victory causes a sensation, and Roxane's duenna brings him a message from her mistress, asking him to meet her in the morning. As he agrees, he learns that Ligniere has offended a powerful nobleman with his latest satire and that a hundred men are waiting to ambush him on his way home. Cyrano boldly proclaims that he will see Ligniere safely home and, if necessary, fight all hundred men in the process.

The next morning, Cyrano meets Roxane at Ragueneau's pastry shop. He nearly tells her his feelings, but she confides in him that she loves Christian, who will soon join Cyrano's company of guards, the Cadets of Gascoyne. She asks Cyrano to protect Christian, and he agrees. Outside, a crowd has gathered, buzzing with the news about Cyrano's triumphs the night before. Cyrano angrily ignores them, upset by his meeting with Roxane. When the cadets arrive, Christian tries to prove his courage by insulting Cyrano's nose—an act generally considered fatal. Instead of killing Christian, however, Cyrano embraces him and tells him about Roxane's feelings. Delighted at first, Christian then becomes distraught. He considers Roxane an intellectual and sees himself as a simple, unpoetic man. Then Cyrano has a bright idea: Cyrano can write to Roxane pretending to be Christian. Christian agrees, welcoming the opportunity to reach Roxane's heart. Now, Cyrano can express all his thoughts and feelings secretly.

One night soon after, Roxane confides in Cyrano that she thinks Christian is the most ravishing poet in the world. Cyrano's disguised letters have moved her inexpressibly. Christian tells Cyrano he no longer wants Cyrano's help, and then makes a fool of himself trying to speak seductively to Roxane. Roxane storms into her house, confused and angry. Thinking quickly, Cyrano makes Christian stand in front of Roxane's balcony and speak to her while Cyrano stands under the balcony whispering to Christian what to say. Eventually, Cyrano shoves Christian aside and, under cover of darkness, pretends to be Christian, wooing Roxane himself. In the process, he wins a kiss for Christian. Roxane and Christian are secretly married by a Capuchin, but their happiness is short-lived: de Guiche, angry to have lost Roxane, declares that he is sending the Cadets of Gascoyne to the front lines of the war with Spain.

At the siege of Arras, the cadets languish and suffer from hunger. Cyrano writes to Roxane every single day, using Christian's name. Moreover, he risks his life each morning by sneaking through the Spanish lines to a place where he can send the letters. De Guiche reveals that the Spaniards will attack within the hour. Suddenly, a coach arrives and Roxane climbs out of it. She has longed to see Christian, again and brings a feast to the soldiers. But Christian has guessed Cyrano's secret feelings for Roxane, and he forces Cyrano to tell her the truth and make her choose between them. On the cusp of revealing his feelings, Cyrano is interrupted by a sudden gunshot that kills Christian. Cyrano cannot tell Roxane the truth. She faints, and de Guiche redeems himself by taking her to safety while Cyrano charges into the battle.

Fifteen years later, Roxane lives in a convent, and Cyrano visits her every week. His friend Le Bret informs Roxane that Cyrano is doing very poorly—he has made many powerful enemies, and his life is constantly in danger. Then, Ragueneau rushes in and privately tells Le Bret that Cyrano has been ambushed and hit with a heavy log pushed out of a high window. His health severely jeopardized, Cyrano could die by simply raising his head from his pillow. Le Bret and Ragueneau rush off to their friend's side. No sooner have they gone than Cyrano appears at the convent, walking slowly and with a pained expression on his face, but sounding as cheerful as ever. He gives Roxane a news update.

As night falls, Cyrano asks to read Christian's last letter to her. He reads it, and when it is completely dark, he continues to read, as if he knows the letter by heart. Roxane realizes that Cyrano wrote the letters—she has found the soul she was in love with all along. Upset, Ragueneau and Le Bret rush in, proclaiming that Cyrano has killed himself by getting out of bed. Cyrano removes his hat, revealing his heavily bandaged head. Roxane exclaims that she loves him and that he cannot die. But Cyrano draws his sword and engages in one last fight with his "old enemies"—falsehood, prejudice, and compromise—slashing at the air insensibly. Then he collapses and dies, smiling as Roxane bends over him and kisses his face.

CHARACTER LIST

Cyrano de Bergerac A poet, swordsman, scientist, playwright, musician, and member of the Cadets of Gascoyne, a company of guards from Southern France. For all his prodigious talents, Cyrano is unattractive, cursed with a ridiculously long nose that makes him insecure and keeps him from revealing his love for his cousin Roxane.

Roxane Cyrano's cousin, a beautiful and intellectual heiress. She has a soft spot for romance and a love for poetry and wit.

Baron Christian de Neuvillette Perhaps the opposite of Cyrano, Christian a handsome but simple young nobleman who lacks wit and intelligence. New to Paris and to the cadets, he falls in love with Roxane and joins Cyrano's company of cadets early in the play. His good looks are matched only by Roxane's.

Comte de Guiche A powerful, married nobleman in love with Roxane and not fond of Cyrano. Deceitful and always angry, he attempts several times to have Cyrano killed, once by a hundred men.

Ragueneau Cyrano's friend, a pastry chef with a deep love for poetry. Ragueneau gives away pastries in return for poems, and, therefore, innumerable poets visit him frequently. He reflects the theme that poetry is food for the soul, and underlines the division between the physical and spiritual aspects of the world. After his business fails, he becomes Roxane's porter.

Le Bret Cyrano's friend and closest confidant. He is a fellow soldier and guardsman. Le Bret worries that Cyrano's principles will ruin his career, but Cyrano ignores Le Bret's concerns.

CHARACTER LIST

Ligniere Christian's friend, a satirist and drunkard with many powerful enemies. Cyrano protects him from the hundred men hired by de Guiche to ambush him.

The duenna Roxane's companion and chaperone,who tries to keep Roxane out of trouble. She is a character reminiscent of Juliet's nurse in *Romeo and Juliet.*

Vicomte de Valvert An insolent young nobleman lauded by de Guiche as a possible husband for Roxane, a scheme that would give de Guiche access to Roxane. After he insults Cyrano's nose, he is defeated in an ensuing duel.

Montfleury A fat, untalented actor whom Cyrano bans from the stage.

Carbon de Castel-Jaloux Cyrano's friend and the captain of his company. He is a strong-willed and successful leader.

Bellerose The man in charge of the theater at the Hotel de Bourgogne.

Lise Ragueneau's sharp-tongued wife. She does not approve of her husband's patronage of the local poets. An altogether unhappy woman, she leaves Ragueneau for a musketeer after Act II.

Capuchin A modest and well-meaning monk. De Guiche employs him to carry a message to Roxane. He is diverted at first by Cyrano when they are outside Roxane's residence. He later presides over Roxane and Christian's hasty wedding.

Mother Marguerite de Jesus, Sister Claire, Sister Marthe Nuns of Roxane's convent. They are compassionate women who admire and respect Cyrano and therefore allow him to visit whenever he wishes.

Cardinal Richelieu Not a character, but a historical figure referenced in the play as de Guiche's uncle. Perhaps the most powerful man in France, he is a skilled political manipulator whose authority rivals and probably exceeds that of the king.

ANALYSIS OF MAJOR CHARACTERS

CYRANO

Cyrano is courageous, poetic, witty, and eloquent. He is a remarkable fighter, poet, musician, and philosopher, as well as a lover of beauty, ideals, and values. Never presented in a bad or unflattering light, Cyrano is difficult to dislike. Throughout the play, Cyrano acts according to his uncompromising sense of values and morals. He remains steadfast in his pursuit to become an honorable man and comes to represent the kind of man that everyone would like to be—and more.

Cyrano displays bravado reminiscent of the warrior tradition, never talking himself or others out of a fight. Cyrano's brashness has earned him many enemies. His lack of self-confidence and low self-esteem, however, prove to be his most potent adversaries. More powerful than the simple flaw from which they grew—his nose—Cyrano's insecurities prevent him from attaining what he cherishes most: love. His inner beauty wins over everyone, but he, and only he, fails to forget about his large nose. In public, Cyrano appears heroic, possessed of an extraordinary wit and a dizzying array of skills. His private self, however, is dark and despondent. Rather than marring his image, the few flaws that Cyrano possesses appear so fundamental to the human condition that they evoke an even deeper appreciation of his character.

Cyrano never wavers in his commitment to Roxane, but he may not be truly in love with her. Perhaps he is in love with the idea of love and of being in love. After all, Cyrano worships and obeys the magic, mystery, and poetry of love, as well as the powers and art of romance. Delighted by the romantic challenge of dying for love, Cyrano allows love to kill him in the end, even after Roxane discovers and reciprocates his feelings.

ROXANE

Cyrano's plot revolves around the effort, by many men, to win Roxane's love. With little agency, curiosity, or will in regard to the entreaties of her suitors, Roxane is the constant star in a perplexing galaxy of affection. Nearly every character is either directly affected by her love or is hoping to win it. But winning *Roxane* is not Cyrano's or Christian's goal: winning her love. It alters Christian and Cyrano in respectively different ways throughout the play, and it defines each scene's tone and attitude.

Roxane's kindness and sincerity never waver and are never questioned. But she has a major dramatic shift in thought at the war at Arras when she tells Christian that although she once loved him because he was handsome, she now loves him because of his inner beauty. This shift alters the play's remaining action and resolves its main action and conflict. Roxane exhibits the sheer power of love over attraction, both at Arras and in the play's final scene, when she declares her love for the deformed Cyrano.

DE GUICHE

De Guiche is an opposing double to Cyrano. He represents everything that Cyrano would become if Cyrano were to use his wit for flattery and social climbing. De Guiche is a violent, vengeful, and bitter man. As the play's villain, he constantly plans to have Cyrano killed, and he is unafraid to admit it.

He serves as a symbol of misguided aristocracy and ineffective leadership. His troops do not respect him. They approve of him only late in the play, when he leads a complex military maneuver for the French and then helps rescue Roxane from the dangers of battle. He does become a better person near the end of the play—a change stemming from Cyrano's remarkable example of kindness, heroism, and respectability.

CHRISTIAN

Christian represents the other half of the romantic hero. He operates as Cyrano's spokesman and comes to represent the shallowness of outer beauty. His good looks and charm tend to overshadow his lingering shyness, waning creativity, and eloquence. Christian's needs and desires are simple and clear com-

CHARACTER ANALYSIS

pared to Cyrano's more complex motivations and goals. Yet there is an undeniable, human source to Christian's deeper emotions and feelings. He is a legitimate lover, but he has no talents to express his love. Christian proves to be rather average in all but his striking physical attractiveness.

THEMES, MOTIFS & SYMBOLS

THEMES

Themes are the fundamental and often universal ideas explored in a literary work.

VALUES AND VIRTUE

Cyrano de Bergerac places strong emphasis on values and ideals. Cyrano is the play's eloquent and ardent defender of integrity, bravery, glory, and the pursuit of love and women. The play's main conflict—Cyrano's inability to tell Roxane how much he loves her out of deference to her request that he protect Christian—results from Cyrano's unwavering promise to keep his word. Cyrano protects his secret nearly to his death; his death itself, though tragic, is also transcendent. The play suggests that by adhering to his values at the expense of his personal desire, Cyrano achieves an ideal, untarnished moral standing. Roxane herself is, in all ways, the ideal woman: she is intelligent, warm, caring, and beautiful.

INNER AND OUTER BEAUTY

Cyrano de Bergerac can be read as an allegory of inner and outer beauty. Cyrano, representing inner beauty, passively battles Christian, who represents outer beauty, for Roxane's love. Roxane becomes the arbiter of the relative values of these characters and, by extension, of the values of inner and outer beauty. The play places a premium on inner beauty, integrity, and intellect. Yet Cyrano's own swashbuckling, flamboyant character emphasizes his exterior rather than his interior traits.

What impresses Roxane and the other marquises is his ability to craft words deftly, to fight off unbelievable numbers of men, and to engage in brilliant gestures: throwing a bag of gold in the theater to pay for the night's receipts and to stop the play; denying himself everything but the most meager meal out of respect for his own pride; and composing a poem to accompany his sword fighting. All of these actions are publicly impressive and derive their power from their outward manifestation. Cyrano's and Christian's outer beauties differ, of course: Christian is blessed with good looks while Cyrano's bombast is a product of a clever mind. Nonetheless, when Roxane claims to be choosing between the outer beauty of Christian and the inner beauty of Cyrano, in many ways she is simply choosing between two different versions of an ostentatious, visible show.

THE DANGER IN DECEPTION

Cyrano is in some ways a morally unblemished character, never veering from his strict moral standards. The play, however, seems to have a moral code that is even stricter than Cyrano's own. Indeed, his one minor flaw—his willingness to deceive Roxane in order to to help Christian, and perhaps even to win her love himself—prevents him from having her at all. Because Cyrano deceives Roxane even after Christian's death, he cannot declare his love for her. Doing so would show disrespect for Christian's memory and make a mockery of her mourning. After Christian's death, the play examines the repercussions of Christian and Cyrano's duplicity by demonstrating the harsh existence that Cyrano must endure: living in close proximity to his one true love, but remaining emotionally barred from her. Through their deception, the two men have made Roxane fall in love with someone who does not exist: an ideal. As a result, she truly loves neither Christian nor Cyrano—she loves their magnificent collaboration. Cyrano and Roxane are never able to consummate the deep love that they undeniably share for each other.

MOTIFS

Motifs are recurring structures, contrasts, or literary devices that can help to develop and inform the text's major themes.

SOCIETY

The first few scenes of Cyrano de Bergerac demonstrate the fallen grace of French society during Rostand's time. In the late nineteenth century, Rostand felt that the French people had forgotten the values and ideals that made them a proud and virtuous people, the qualities and character that made them honorable and specifically French. The critique of society continues in the presentation of several peripheral characters. De Guiche is a corrupted, powerful man who fails to win the respect that a leader should. Lise is unfaithful to her husband and leaves him to seek sensual adventure.

THE LETTERS

Cyrano is constantly composing, whether he writes ballads as he fights, recites poetry in the dark, or writes love letters for Christian. His compositions are not just literary; they also represent a way for Cyrano to create an identity for himself that he feels he can never have in real life. The letters in which he declares his love for Roxane begin to replace Cyrano himself. However, they also reveal a failing on Cyrano's part: just as Christian cannot express himself in words, Cyrano cannot express himself in action. The only action he undertakes to win Roxane's heart is this deceptive composing. The letters become inseparable from Cyrano's inner beauty.

FIGHTING AND WAR

Many characters in the play are fighters, whether they are members of the cadets or the musketeers. In the first three acts, these characters display their strengths and settle their arguments with swords. The play has a violent twist. When the play presents the war in Act IV, much of the play's tension begins to heighten, and the climax suddenly occurs: Christian dies in Roxane's arms while Cyrano looks on. After this heart-wrenching scene, most of the play's force, or conflict, dissolves, and the characters return to their lives however they may have changed.

SYMBOLS

Symbols are objects, characters, figures, or colors used to represent abstract ideas or concepts.

CYRANO'S NOSE

Cyrano's nose is the most obvious symbol in the play. Not only does it make him ugly, it characterizes Cyrano's main flaw: his lack of self-confidence and initiative in potential encounters with love, and the deceptive actions he commits as a consequence of this low self-esteem. His nose is the barrier between him and love. Every time he opens his eyes, the nose is there, stretching out into his field of vision. As the play progresses, Cyrano's nose might also be a symbol for society's reliance on outer beauty, and its inability to see inner beauty.

CYRANO'S TEARS AND CHRISTIAN'S BLOOD

In Act V, when Roxane realizes Cyrano's secret, she notices that the tears on Christian's letter are probably Cyrano's tears. Cyrano responds by deflecting her comment and stating that the blood is Christian's. This mixture of blood and tears on the final letter symbolizes the melding of Cyrano and Christian into the romantic hero. This combination helps Roxane realize their deception.

Summary & Analysis

Act I, scenes i–iii

> VALVERT: *Your nose is . . . very big.*
> CYRANO: *Yes, very.*   (See QUOTATIONS, p. 43)

SUMMARY — ACT I, SCENE I
In the year 1640, the Hall of the Hotel de Bourgogne—a large, crowded Parisian theater—buzzes with activity in the minutes before a performance of the play *La Clorise*. People mill about and converse, divided according to their social class. A citizen guides his son through the room, impressing upon him the intellectual magnitude of the performance. A thief moves through the crowd, stealing handkerchiefs and purses. A group of pages runs about firing peashooters at one another. Two elegant marquises, with swords strapped to their waists, tread through the crowd, aloof and condescending. The lamps are lit, and the crowd cheers, knowing the performance will commence soon.

SUMMARY — ACT I, SCENE II
The audience waits for the play to begin. The disheveled satirist Ligniere enters, arm in arm, with the handsome young nobleman Baron Christian de Neuvillette, who tells a group of admiring marquises that he has been in Paris only two or three weeks and that he will join the guards tomorrow. Ligniere has come to report to Christian about the woman with whom Christian has fallen in love. Christian says she is always at the plays. But she has not arrived yet, and Ligniere prepares to leave—he says he needs to find a tavern. When a refreshment girl passes by with wine, Ligniere agrees to stay. Ragueneau, a baker who caters to and idolizes poets, enters, looking for Cyrano de Bergerac. He says he expects trouble because an actor named Montfleury is performing in the play. He knows Cyrano hates Montfleury and has banned him from performing onstage for a month.

Christian has never heard of Cyrano de Bergerac, but Ragueneau and Ligniere seem to be almost in awe of him. Christian asks who Cyrano is, and his friend Le Bret says that Cyrano is the "most delightful man under the sun." The others describe him as a poet, swordsman, scientist, musician, and "wild swashbuckler" with a long sword. They also say he has an unbelievably long and imposing nose. But he is a formidable figure, and Le Bret, who serves with Cyrano in the guards, says he too expects trouble.

Suddenly, Christian spies the woman with whom he has fallen in love. Ligniere tells him that she is Roxane, a brilliant, young heiress and intellectual. She sits in a box with a somewhat older man—the Comte de Guiche, who is also in love with her. Ligniere says the Comte is married and hopes to marry Roxane to his lackey, the Vicomte de Valvert. Christian is most upset to learn that Roxane is an intellectual. Ligniere leaves to find a tavern, and there is still no sign of Cyrano. The crowd grows anxious for the play to begin.

SUMMARY — ACT I, SCENE III

The two marquises discuss de Guiche distastefully as he walks toward them. Christian observes their exchange. Christian decides to challenge de Guiche's lackey, Valvert, to a duel; as he reaches for his glove, with which he plans to challenge Valvert by slapping him in the face with it, he catches the hand of a pickpocket. In exchange for his release, the thief tells Christian that Ligniere's latest satire has offended a powerful man, who has arranged for Ligniere to be ambushed by a hundred men later that night on his way home. Christian leaves to save Ligniere.

The crowd begins to chant for the play. Three raps sound from the stage, and the crowd becomes quiet. The curtains open. The violins play. Le Bret and Ragueneau decide that Cyrano must not be in the audience since Montfleury, the actor whom Cyrano detests, is about to make his entrance. Dressed as a shepherd, the pudgy actor walks onto the stage and begins to deliver a speech. Suddenly, a voice from the crowd cries out, "Haven't I ordered you off the stage for a month, you wretched scoundrel?" The speaker is hidden, but Le Bret knows it must be Cyrano. Montfleury makes several attempts to begin his lines, but the heckling speaker continues to interrupt him. Cyrano finally stands upon his chair, and his appearance creates a stir throughout the audience.

ANALYSIS — ACT I, SCENES I–III

This long scene introduces a host of important characters, the main facts of the story, and a suspenseful, miniature story line designed to demonstrate the overwhelming character of Cyrano de Bergerac. The exchanges between the characters in the first two scenes provide the ground for the subsequent action of the play, heightening the suspense surrounding Cyrano's character by keeping him physically absent until just after the performance begins. Cyrano stands apart from the rest of the characters, who appear to be somewhat dull and predictable.

Rostand's play romanticizes an era that was looked upon nostalgically by some nineteenth-century writers. Written around 1897, *Cyrano de Bergerac* is set in 1640. The play is not a realistic interpretation of the time it describes, but rather a historical romance, designed to evoke the glory of France during the age of Louis XIII and to provide an entertaining escape for its audience. The play takes many of its stereotypical representations from Dumas's popular novel *The Three Musketeers*. Several references to Dumas's work appear in the play. In Act I, scene iv, after Cyrano fights in a dramatic duel, his friend Cuigy wittily claims that Cyrano's name is Dartagnan. (D'Artagnan is the hero of Dumas's novel, written 200 years after the time in which *Cyrano de Bergerac* is set.) Later, Le Bret admonishes Cyrano to "stop trying to be Three Musketeers in one!"

The opening scenes emphasize the importance of the theater in seventeenth-century France. The theater patrons include thieves, lackeys, pages, and cavaliers—a veritable cross section of French society at the time. Several patrons come to the theater to do everything but watch the play. Some pick pockets, others play cards, others want to be seen and improve their social status. Rostand parodies inattentive audiences and supposedly bad actors like Montfleury to provide a critique of the theater of *his* era. By opening the play with such a critical portrayal, Rostand captures the audience's attention and subtly encourages them to listen up and behave appropriately.

ACT I, SCENES IV–VII

SUMMARY — ACT I, SCENE IV

Montfleury cries out to the group of marquises for help, and several respond. They try to quiet Cyrano, who invokes several poetic metaphors as he threatens to kill them all: "Please have pity on my sword: if you don't stop shouting you'll frighten it out of its scabbard." As the crowd gasps and strains to see, Cyrano offers a universal challenge to the marquises, saying he will take their names and fight them each in turn. None of the marquises take his challenge. He gives Montfleury to the count of three to leave the stage, and the actor flees.

The crowd is in a tumult. Cyrano proclaims that Montfleury is a horrible actor and that the play is wretched. Moreover, Cyrano says he has personal reasons for forbidding Montfleury to perform. The manager of the stage indignantly asks about the money he will lose from the performance, and Cyrano dramatically tosses him a purse full of gold. A meddler storms up to Cyrano and declares that Montfleury has a powerful patron. Cyrano exclaims that he himself has no patron or any need for one because he can protect himself with his sword. He accuses the meddler of staring at his nose, and he bullies him about the room. Cowed, the meddler insists that he was not staring and suggests that Cyrano's nose is small. Cyrano angrily exclaims that his nose is *magnificent.*

De Guiche declares to Valvert that Cyrano is tiresome. Valvert agrees to put him in his place and, approaching Cyrano, tries to goad him by saying that Cyrano has a "very big" nose. Affecting astonishment at the man's lack of wit, Cyrano offers a long list of better insults that he himself might have used in Valvert's situation. He continues to mock Valvert, who challenges him to a duel. Cyrano declares that as he fights Valvert, he will speak an extemporaneous poem and kill Valvert on the last line.

Enthralled, the crowd forms a ring around the combatants. Cyrano and Valvert draw their swords and begin to fight. As they fight, Cyrano invents a poem that matches exactly the action of the duel. As promised, on the last line of the refrain, he thrusts, and Valvert falls backward, beaten and badly wounded. The crowd cheers ecstatically. Gradually, the crowd disperses for dinner. Le Bret asks Cyrano why he does not go to eat and Cyrano replies that he has no money. Le Bret asks about the purse of gold Cyrano threw to the stage manager, Bellerose, and Cyrano reveals that it was all the money he had and that it should have lasted him for a month. The refreshment girl offers him food. Eager not to injure his pride or betray a lack of respect for the girl's offer, he accepts only one grape, a half of a macaroon, and a glass of water.

Summary — Act I, scene v

Le Bret reminds Cyrano that his extravagant behavior is making him enemies. Cyrano says that the thought of having so many enemies makes him happy. Cyrano confides in Le Bret that he has insecurities concerning his nose and his romantic failures. He also

reveals to Le Bret that he hates Montfleury because one day Montfleury glanced flirtatiously at the woman whom Cyrano loves. Le Bret
asks about the woman but quickly realizes that the only woman
beautiful and brilliant enough for Cyrano to love must be Roxane.
Cyrano says that given his appearance, he can never reveal his love.

SUMMARY — ACT I, SCENE VI
Roxane's duenna appears and interrupts their conversation. She has
a message for Cyrano: Roxane wants to see him. Tremendously
excited, and perhaps a bit nervous, he agrees to meet her at Rag_ue-
neau's shop at seven o'clock the next morning.

SUMMARY — ACT I, SCENE VII
Ligniere rushes in. He tells Cyrano about the hundred men waiting
at the Porte de Nesle to kill him and announces that he is too afraid
to go home. He asks if Cyrano can host him for the evening, but
Cyrano scoffs: "A hundred men, you say?—You'll sleep at home
tonight!" He declares that he will fight all hundred men and escort
Ligniere safely home. Le Bret asks why Cyrano would want to help
a drunkard, and Cyrano says that he once saw Ligniere drink a
whole font of holy water dry after a beautiful woman had blessed
herself with it. For a gesture like that, he says, he will protect
Ligniere.

   The actors and musicians rehearsing in the theater buzz about
Cyrano's behavior. He tells them that he wants an audience and that
they can follow him. But he warns them that he wants no protection.
As he strides boldly out of the theater, the crowd forms a procession
to follow him to the Porte de Nestle.

ANALYSIS — ACT I, SCENES IV–VII
In these scenes, Cyrano appears almost superhuman in his grace,
agility, and wit. He demonstrates his uncanny sense of humor and
his willingness to laugh at himself and his nose. In standing up to
Valvert, he shows off his unparalleled wit, as well as his courage and
strength. His ability to compose a ballad while simultaneously dis-
playing his talent for swordfighting is remarkable. His display of
modesty and humility toward the theater patrons and the refreshment girl shows his gentlemanly nature. Cyrano's unsightly nose
becomes only one of many characteristics that distinguish him from
everyone else in the play. This first act establishes Cyrano as

uniquely gifted and heroic. More than merely a central character, he is a living legend.

Cyrano also shows his humble side in these scenes. He presents his heroism and eclectic skills to the public, and shows his emotional turmoil and self-doubt to his closest friends. He explains to Le Bret that he sometimes becomes depressed because of his nose and because he is not like the other lovers he sees. In some ways, his sense of alienation seems to prompt Cyrano to search for love even more ardently. But he is also unreasonably tough on himself, focusing only on his failures, imperfections, and weaknesses.

Rostand subtitles *Cyrano de Bergerac* a "heroic comedy," a description that applies perfectly to the first act. Cyrano's brash, arrogant behavior is so astonishing that his ridiculously long nose, which might otherwise be the defining feature of his character, is humorous only for a moment. The nose becomes another extraordinary feature of this extraordinary character, and we are moved to laugh with Cyrano rather than at him. Rostand successfully diverts the tendency to fixate on Cyrano's odd appearance by emphasizing his extraordinary character instead. Cyrano's countless displays of wit, valor, and heroism—most notably his resolve to defend Ligniere from a hundred men—make him into an exaggerated stereotype of the swashbuckling, seventeenth-century poet-cavalier.

There is an inherent parallel between the audience in the Hotel de Bourgogne and the audience watching (or reading) Rostand's play. The reactions of the crowd enable us to sense the scope and magnitude of Cyrano's feats. They shout platitudes and celebratory adjectives that help put Cyrano's feats into perspective, evoking a sense of immediacy and presence.

Act II, scenes i–vi

> *His face shines with wit and intelligence. He's proud, noble, young, fearless, handsome. . . .*
> (See QUOTATIONS, p. 44)

Summary — Act II, scene i

The next morning dawns. The scene is Ragueneau's bakery. The bakery bustles with activity as Ragueneau and his pastry cooks prepare the day's wares. Obsessed with poetry, Ragueneau has written all of his recipes in the form of poems. One of the cooks delights him with a pastry lyre.

Ragueneau's wife, Lise, enters furiously, angry with Ragueneau for yet again giving away baked goods to poets in return for their verses. She shows him a new batch of paper bags she has made for the shop, shocking her husband because the bags are made from poet's manuscripts.

Summary — Act II, scene ii

Two children enter the shop and order three small pies. Ragueneau struggles to find a bag, and a poem, with which he can part. After Lise is out of sight, Ragueneau brings the children back and offers to give them more pastries if they will return the bags that have poetry written on them.

Summary — Act II, scene iii

Cyrano appears and tells Ragueneau he is meeting someone. Noticeably nervous and jumpy, Cyrano constantly asks what time it is and cannot sit still. Lise asks Cyrano how he cut his hand, but he refuses to talk about it. A musketeer arrives and Ragueneau says the man is his wife's friend.

Summary — Act II, scene iv

Some poets arrive and begin eating Ragueneau's wares, describing the food poetically and thereby delighting the baker. Cyrano tries to write something to Roxane. When Ragueneau leaves, Cyrano warns Lise that Ragueneau is his friend and that he will not tolerate her having an affair with the musketeer. The musketeer hears what he says but does not dare to challenge Cyrano.

Summary — Act II, scene v

Roxane arrives. Overcome with love, Cyrano sends everyone else away. He gives the duenna pastries to distract her while he and Roxane spend time together.

Summary — Act II, scene vi

Cyrano and Roxane begin to talk alone. Cyrano anxiously asks Roxane to state why she has come to talk to him. She shrugs off his insistence, and they reminisce about the childhood summers they spent together. She tends to his wounded hand, and Cyrano tells her he injured it in a fight the night before in which he defeated a hundred men. Roxane confesses to Cyrano that she is in love with someone, a man who does not know she loves him. Cyrano thinks she means him, but when she describes the man as "handsome," he knows that she means someone else. She tells him that she is in love with Christian, the new member of Cyrano's company of guards. She says that she is afraid for Christian because Cyrano's company is composed of hot-blooded Gascons who pick fights with anyone foreign. Christian is not a Gascon. Roxane asks Cyrano to protect him, and Cyrano agrees. She also asks Cyrano to have Christian write to her. Professing friendly love and admiration for Cyrano, she leaves.

ANALYSIS — ACT II, SCENES I–VI

In *Cyrano de Bergerac,* poetry either splits lovers apart or binds them together. Poetry divides Ragueneau and Lise, providing the main conflict in their marriage. Whereas Ragueneau is a caring, compassionate individual with a weakness for poets and poetry, Lise, his domineering wife, disparages poetry, pasting old pages of poems together to make bags for the shop. Her disgust becomes even more obvious when her affair with the musketeer becomes apparent. Ragueneau risks his business and his marriage by constantly giving out large amounts of pastries in return for poems. Meanwhile, the power of poetry will soon begin to bring other lovers together, and Ragueneau's poetic shop will play an important role in that process. In this scene, the sequence of letter-writing that continues through the rest of the play begins when Roxane and Cyrano meet in Ragueneau's shop.

Cyrano once again exhibits his greatest strengths and weaknesses within the same scene. He stands up for Ragueneau's honor by threatening Lise and the musketeer. Cyrano will not allow them to deceive Ragueneau while they continue their dishonorable affair. Cyrano may not cherish Ragueneau's poems, but he respects his character and the goodwill he shows to him and to the other poets. Cyrano's fragility comes across in his nervousness during his meeting with Roxane. Cyrano is often courageous and fearless, but not when it comes to love. Despite his remarkable talents and abilities, he has the self-doubt and sense of vulnerability common to almost everyone.

When Roxane arrives, it seems as though Cyrano's dream has come true. She begins to talk about a love interest of hers, and throughout her lengthy and somewhat stealthy description of the man, Cyrano appears to believe that she is talking about him. When she says that this man is "handsome," Cyrano concludes that the man cannot be him, highlighting one of his most profound and destructive flaws—lack of self-esteem. Cyrano soon convinces himself that Roxane will never reciprocate his love. Sad and despondent, Cyrano resolves to help Christian win her heart. Cyrano's resolve, as well as his promise to protect Christian, demonstrates his essential heroic qualities. He combats rejection and dejection with selfless love—perhaps Cyrano's most impressive quality displayed thus far.

Act II, scenes VII–XI

> *Will you let my soul pass from my leather jerkin and*
> *lodge beneath your embroidered doublet?*
> (See QUOTATIONS, p. 45)

Summary — Act II, scene VII

Cyrano's company of guards tumbles into the shop, ecstatic over Cyrano's triumphs the night before. The whole city is in a tumult over the sensation he created. Carbon, the captain of the guards, tries to lead Cyrano out into the adoring throng, but Cyrano refuses to go. People begin rushing into the store, doting on Cyrano. Prominent men ask for the details of the night before; Cyrano's friends see an opportunity for him to help his career, but he refuses to provide any details. De Guiche enters with a message of admiration, and Cyrano presents to him the song of the Cadets of Gascoyne. De Guiche suggests that his uncle, Cardinal Richelieu, the most powerful man in France, might be willing to help Cyrano. But again Cyrano refuses. During the hubbub, a cadet appears with a set of hats belonging to the men Cyrano defeated the previous night. De Guiche reveals that he hired the hundred men, and he angrily storms out of the store. The crowd dissipates, and only the guards remain.

Summary — Act II, scene VIII

Le Bret argues that Cyrano is ruining his chances of becoming a successful man or a famous poet. Cyrano says he will live according to his ideals and that he has no interest in making friends with unworthy men. Suddenly, Christian enters.

SUMMARY & ANALYSIS

SUMMARY & ANALYSIS

SUMMARY — ACT II, SCENE IX

The other guardsmen, not privy to Cyrano's vow to Roxane, tease Christian and warn him never to mention Cyrano's nose. Christian, upset that he is being teased, asks Carbon what to do when Gascons grow too boastful. Carbon replies that he must prove a man can be a Norman and still have courage. So when Cyrano begins to tell the story of his fight with the hundred men, Christian repeatedly interrupts him with references to his nose. Cyrano fills with anger, and the cadets expect him to attack Christian. Remembering his promise to protect Christian, however, Cyrano controls himself. Christian's insults continue until at last Cyrano angrily sends away the cadets. Expecting him to kill Christian, they hasten from the room.

SUMMARY — ACT II, SCENE X

Rather than killing Christian, Cyrano embraces him and reveals that he is Roxane's cousin. Christian proclaims that he simply cannot write to Roxane because he is too stupid—he thinks she will lose all feeling for him the moment she reads his words. Struck by a powerful idea, Cyrano offers to write letters *for* Christian—though he says he is only interested in practicing his comic poetry, inwardly, he burns for the opportunity to express his feelings to Roxane. Christian agrees, and they embrace again.

SUMMARY — ACT II, SCENE XI

The cadets return to the room, stunned to see that not only is Christian still alive, but that he is embracing Cyrano. Lise's musketeer decides to follow Christian's lead and insults Cyrano's nose. Cyrano knocks him over a bench. The cadets, pleased to have their old Cyrano back, rejoice.

———————————

ANALYSIS — ACT II, SCENES VII–XI

The structure of Act II is important for several reasons. It introduces the plot's main event: Cyrano's plan to woo Roxane for Christian by writing the letters himself. It shows Cyrano at the peak of his sensational popularity following his triumph at the theater and in the duel against a hundred men. It also shows how his pride and virtue compel him to shun his popularity.

Rostand expresses in words the code of behavior to which Cyrano swears. Cyrano's refusal of Richelieu's patronage is significant.

Rather than pander to money and power by taking a great offer to become financially and politically backed by the most powerful man in France, Cyrano prefers to live by the ideals and values that he holds dear. Moreover, Cyrano's argument with Le Bret over Cyrano's rash behavior shows his allegiance to integrity, impetuousness, bravery, wit, the pursuit of glory, and the idealization of love and women—all in the face of great enmity. These connote the most important, recurring themes of the play.

Another important theme of *Cyrano de Bergerac* is the traditional contrast between inner worth and outward appearance, embodied mainly in the opposing characters of Cyrano and Christian. Christian and Cyrano are opposites in several ways. One is ugly, the other handsome. One is smart and artistic, the other simple. One is confident, the other noticeably shy but effectively charming. Cyrano, despite his awkward physical appearance, is the "most delightful man under the sun," a consistently brilliant and soulful man. Christian is beautiful to look at, but he lacks wit, poetry, and fire. By working together to woo Roxane, they form a more powerful single character, a "romantic hero." This romantic hero has the best of both worlds: Cyrano's inner beauty and Christian's outer beauty. Though together they form a romantic hero, Cyrano and Christian also risk becoming perceived as part fraud and part coward.

ACT III, SCENES I–IV

SUMMARY — ACT III, SCENE I

Ragueneau sits outside Roxane's house conversing with her duenna. He tells the duenna that his wife, Lise, ran off with a musketeer and that his bakery is ruined. He says that he tried to hang himself but that Cyrano found him, cut him down, and made him Roxane's steward. The duenna calls up to Roxane, telling her to hurry. They are going to a discussion group on the tender passion. Cyrano strides into the scene followed by a pair of musicians, whose services he won in a bet over a fine point of grammar. The musicians are terrible, however, and Cyrano sends them off to play an out-of-tune serenade to Montfleury.

Roxane comes down, and she and Cyrano talk about Christian. Roxane says that Christian's letters have been breathtaking—he is more intellectual than even Cyrano, she declares. Moreover, she says that she loves Christian. She recites passages of the letters to

Cyrano, who makes a show of critiquing the poetry. Roxane says that Cyrano is jealous of Christian's poetic talent. The duenna cries out that de Guiche is coming, and Cyrano, hastened by the duenna, hides inside the house.

SUMMARY — ACT III, SCENE II

De Guiche tells Roxane that he has come to say farewell. He has been made a colonel of an army regiment that is leaving that night to fight in the war with Spain. He mentions that the regiment includes Cyrano's guards, and he grimly predicts that he and Cyrano will have a reckoning. Afraid for Christian's safety if he should go to the front, Roxane quickly suggests that the best way for de Guiche to seek revenge on Cyrano would be for him to leave Cyrano and his cadets behind while the rest of the regiment goes on to military glory. After much flirtation from Roxane, de Guiche believes he should stay close by, concealed in a local monastery. When Roxane implies that she would feel more for de Guiche if he went to war, he agrees to march on steadfastly, leaving Cyrano and his cadets behind. He leaves, and Roxane makes the duenna promise she will not tell Cyrano that Roxane has robbed him of a chance to go to war.

SUMMARY — ACT III, SCENE III

Roxane expects Christian to come visit her, and she tells the duenna to make him wait if he does. Cyrano presses Roxane to disclose that instead of questioning Christian on any particular subject, she plans to make Christian improvise about love. Cyrano agrees that he will not tell Christian the details of her plot, a gesture Roxane appreciates. She conjectures that Christian would prepare a speech to her if he knew. Roxane and the duenna leave, and Cyrano calls to Christian, who has been waiting nearby.

SUMMARY — ACT III, SCENE IV

Cyrano tries to help Christian prepare for his meeting with Roxane. He urges Christian to learn lines Cyrano has written. But Christian refuses. He says he wants to speak to Roxane in his own words, and Cyrano bows to Christian, saying, "Speak for yourself, sir."

ANALYSIS — ACT III, SCENES I–IV

Rostand's play does not hold musketeers in high esteem. This dislike becomes immediately apparent when the distasteful Lise runs away with one. Many of the references to the musketeers and to Dumas's *The Three Musketeers* are overwhelmingly negative. By this point, the musketeers have been developed as symbols of an antiquated and corrupt past. Rostand uses the musketeers as moral foils, contrasting them with more noble characters, such as Cyrano, Roxane, and even Christian. For instance, when Lise's despicable actions with the musketeer drive Ragueneau to desperate measures, Cyrano saves Ragueneau's life, consoles him, and finds him a job. Cyrano cleans up the mess made by the musketeers.

Cyrano's development as a heroic and moral character becomes even more remarkable in these scenes. He displays his knowledge of music, language, and mathematics. Despite his affection for Roxane, Cyrano enjoys helping Christian win her love, a fact that exemplifies Cyrano's attraction to challenges of all kinds. But he also displays modesty: when Roxane praises the letters, which he secretly wrote, Cyrano does not believe that they have truly affected her. He realizes this impact, or allows himself to realize it, only when Roxane recites many of the lines back to him by heart. Cyrano may be proud, but he is also unbelievably humble.

These scenes present Roxane as an expert moderator who has powerful skills of persuasion. First, she convinces Cyrano about the beauty of the letters. But her most important achievement is persuading de Guiche to forgo taking vengeance upon Cyrano. Perhaps de Guiche's reluctance can be attributed to his feelings for Roxane, but it is her persuasive flirting that clearly affects him.

The contrast between Cyrano and Christian intensifies in these scenes: Cyrano is humble and reserved, and Christian is proud and supremely confident, yet simple-minded. Given Cyrano's incomparable love for Roxane, his ability to maintain a strong sense of reserve as she compliments the letters is remarkable. In comparison, Christian is more excited than Cyrano, though he did not even write the letters. At the end of scene iv, Christian seems somewhat unappreciative of Cyrano and believes the wooing is complete. Christian doesn't understand that his decision to speak to Roxane without Cyrano's help might lead him down a difficult and disastrous path.

ACT III, SCENES V–XIV

SUMMARY — ACT III, SCENE V

Roxane and the duenna return. Roxane and Christian sit out-
doors, and Roxane asks Christian to tell her how he loves her. He
tries, but all he can say is "I love you," "I adore you," "I love you
very much," and other simple variations. Angry, Roxane goes into
the house. Cyrano returns, ironically congratulating Christian on
his great success.

SUMMARY — ACT III, SCENE VI

Seeing a light in Roxane's window, Christian asks Cyrano for help.
In the dark, Cyrano hides underneath Roxane's balcony while
Christian stands in front of it. He throws gravel at Roxane's window, and when she comes out, Cyrano whispers words for Christian
to recite.

SUMMARY — ACT III, SCENE VII

Moved by Christian's words, Roxane then asks why he speaks so
haltingly. Impatient, Cyrano thrusts Christian under the balcony
and takes his place, still hidden in darkness. Speaking in a low voice,
he confides in Roxane the things he has always longed to tell her. As
Roxane becomes more and more hypnotized by Cyrano's poetry,
Christian cries out from beneath the balcony that he wants one kiss.
At first, Cyrano tries to dissuade him, but he decides that he cannot
prevent the inevitable and that, at the very least, he would like to be
the one to win the kiss. Thus, Cyrano stands beneath Roxane's balcony and persuades her to kiss him. Christian climbs up to receive
the kiss.

SUMMARY — ACT III, SCENE VIII

A Capuchin priest enters, having found his way to Roxane's house.
He presents a letter from de Guiche. The letter says that de Guiche
has escaped his military service by hiding in a convent. Pretending to
read it aloud, Roxane says that de Guiche desires the Capuchin to
marry Roxane and Christian on the spot. The Capuchin hesitates,
but Roxane pretends to discover a postscript that promises a great
deal of money to the convent in exchange. Suddenly, the Capuchin's
reservations evaporate, and he goes inside to marry them.

SUMMARY & ANALYSIS

SUMMARY — ACT III, SCENE IX

Cyrano waits outside to prevent de Guiche from disrupting the impromptu wedding.

SUMMARY — ACT III, SCENE X

De Guiche appears. Covering his face with his hat, Cyrano leaps onto de Guiche from a tree. Pretending to be a person who has just fallen from the moon, he distracts de Guiche with an insane speech about his experiences in space. At last he removes his hat, reveals himself as Cyrano, and announces that Roxane and Christian are now married.

SUMMARY — ACT III, SCENE XI

The couple comes out of the house. De Guiche coldly congratulates them but orders Roxane to bid her husband farewell: the guards will go to the war after all, and they will depart immediately. De Guiche triumphantly tells Cyrano that the wedding night will have to wait. Under his breath, Cyrano remarks that the news fails to upset him.

Roxane, afraid for Christian, urges Cyrano to promise to keep him safe, to keep him out of dangerous situations, to keep him dry and warm, and to keep him faithful. Cyrano says that he will do what he can but that he cannot promise anything. Roxane begs Cyrano to promise to make Christian write to her every day. Brightening, Cyrano announces confidently that he can promise that.

ANALYSIS — ACT III, SCENES V–XIV

The balcony scene is the most famous scene in *Cyrano de Bergerac*. It is at once brilliantly funny and genuinely touching. The humor of the play becomes more sophisticated in Act III. In the earlier parts of the play, most of the humor stems from Cyrano's outrageous behavior. Here, the humor begins to take the form of elaborate dramatic irony. (Dramatic irony is a literary device that occurs when the audience knows or perceives more than the characters do.) For example, Roxane believes Cyrano to be Christian, and de Guiche doesn't recognize Cyrano when he claims to have fallen from space. The comic timing in this act is flawless. Cyrano's aside about how he secretly does not mind that the wedding night will be delayed comes at just the right moment. Another important source of humor in Act III is parody: the balcony scene derives a great deal of its humor by ridiculing the famous balcony scene in *Romeo and Juliet*.

De Guiche, the play's main antagonist, begins to influence the plot directly in this act. In Act I, de Guiche was in love with Roxane. Now, he takes steps to fulfill his love. At first, Roxane and Cyrano thwart those attempts. Roxane bribes the Capuchin, and Cyrano distracts de Guiche with his spaceman ploy. But de Guiche's decision to send the cadets to war throws the whole plot into upheaval. De Guiche himself represents another reference to *The Three Muske-teers*: in that play, Cardinal Richelieu is the principal villain, and here, the cardinal's nephew turns into the primary antagonist.

ACT IV, SCENES I–V

Your true self has prevailed over your outer
appearance. I now love you for your soul alone.
(See QUOTATIONS, p. 46)

SUMMARY — ACT IV, SCENE I
At the siege of Arras, the Cadets of Carbon de Castel-Jaloux lan-guish, surrounded by the encamped Spaniards and lacking food and water. Le Bret keeps watch with Carbon early one morning, and they discuss the plight of the soldiers. They hear gunfire in the dis-tance, and Cyrano runs in. Every morning he has been crossing enemy lines to post a daily letter to Roxane. Cyrano tells the startled guards that he promised Roxane that Christian would write her every single day. Cyrano looks at the sleeping Christian and says that Christian is dying of hunger but is still handsome.

SUMMARY — ACT IV, SCENE II
Dawn breaks, drums sound, and Cyrano goes off to write another letter. The cadets awaken and complain about their hunger. There is talk of a mutiny, and Carbon asks Cyrano for his help.

SUMMARY — ACT IV, SCENE III
Cyrano comes out and talks to the cadets, restoring morale with a clever speech and his passionate commitment to the cause. He implores a piper to play a song from Provence, and though the cadets become tearfully homesick, they do forget about their hun-ger. De Guiche enters, evoking a general murmur of resentment from the cadets. Cyrano tells the miserable cadets to stop moping and to look busy as de Guiche arrives.

SUMMARY — ACT IV, SCENE IV

Prompted by Cyrano, de Guiche boasts of his conduct in the previous day's battle when, to confuse the Spaniards, he flung away the white plume that marked him as an officer. Cyrano then proclaims that a courageous man would never have flung away the white plume, and he offers to wear it in the next bout of fighting. De Guiche says Cyrano makes the pledge only because he knows the plume lies somewhere on the battlefield. To the cadets' delight, Cyrano produces the plume from his pocket.

Furious, de Guiche seizes the plume and waves it to a sentry, who runs toward the Spanish encampments. De Guiche says that he has just given a signal and that the Spanish will attack in perhaps an hour. He says that the cadets will all die but that, in the process, they will buy the French forces as much time as possible. Cyrano thanks de Guiche solemnly for the opportunity to die with glory.

Christian tells Cyrano he wishes he could say farewell to Roxane, and Cyrano shows him the farewell letter he has just written. Christian notices the mark of a tear on the letter and nearly guesses Cyrano's secret. He is interrupted by the arrival of a mysterious coach.

SUMMARY — ACT IV, SCENE V

De Guiche thinks that the coach is from the king's service. But Roxane delightfully surprises both him and the other men when she climbs down from the coach. She says that the war was lasting too long and that she had to see Christian. Cyrano, Christian, and de Guiche tell her she must leave immediately because the Spaniards will attack soon. She refuses to leave, saying that she is brave—after all, she is Cyrano's cousin. De Guiche leaves angrily.

ANALYSIS — ACT IV, SCENES I–V

The beginning of Act IV marks a severe shift in tone and sentiment. The cadets, at war, are starving. Their morale is low, and they yearn to return home. Cyrano is the only soldier in decent spirits: his daily writing to Roxane gives him a sense of purpose in the difficult time. De Guiche decides to have his sentry advise the Spanish to attack the cadets, partly in revenge for his humiliation at the hands of Cyrano, but mainly because he needs to buy time as part of a larger military maneuver. Pitted against the overwhelming Spanish force, the cadets will suffer almost certain death.

The jokes in these scenes, while present, add to this shift in tone, providing a sense of unease rather than delight. For instance, while the hungry cadets sleep, Carbon evokes the proverb, "He who sleeps dines." Le Bret agrees, but adds, "That's not much comfort when you have insomnia." Similarly, Cyrano's observation, that Christian might be dying of hunger but still has his good looks, exemplifies a sense of humor that simultaneously creates and stifles laughter.

Still, Cyrano never misses an opportunity to highlight de Guiche's hypocrisy and ignorance, and thus continues to bring a sense of vibrancy and life to the outwardly hopeless situation. The ironic exchange between Cyrano and de Guiche regarding the white plume adds to the impression that de Guiche is an inferior coward and buffoon. Cyrano accomplishes this feat through his use of irony and surprise. Intending to attack de Guiche for his cowardliness eventually, Cyrano prompts de Guiche to begin bragging about how he strategically fooled the enemy in the previous battle. After setting him up, Cyrano can now tear him down, showing not only how de Guiche threw away the symbol of courage, but how Cyrano braved the battlefield to retrieve the white plume.

Indeed, the white plume begins to symbolize idealistic bravery, honor, and glory. Worn by colonels, it serves the practical purpose of signaling to a brigade the whereabouts of the troops' leader. However, it also might leave the colonel vulnerable to personal attack from the opposition. Yet, while de Guiche sees the plume as a limitation and cleverly evades the Spanish threat by casting it aside, Cyrano illustrates that the plume serves a higher purpose, adding respectability and honor to battle, so much so that Cyrano risks his own life to retrieve and honor it. Perhaps more romantic than realistic in nature, the plume and the ideals associated with it serve as a beacon for Cyrano's insurmountable, uncompromising spirit.

ACT IV, SCENES VI–X

SUMMARY — ACT IV, SCENE VI

Carbon presents the company to Roxane, and, to their surprise and delight, she produces Ragueneau—and the feast that he has prepared for the cadets—from the coach. The men gorge themselves, but when de Guiche reappears, they hide the food.

SUMMARY — ACT IV, SCENE VII

De Guiche announces that if Roxane stays for the battle, he will stay to fight as well. The men decide that he must be a Gascon after all, and they offer him some food. He refuses, and they are even more impressed. Cyrano tells Christian that he has written Roxane more often than Christian thought—in fact, every day. Christian again suspects Cyrano's secret, but Roxane interrupts.

SUMMARY — ACT IV, SCENE VIII

Christian asks why Roxane risked death to see him again, and she says that she was driven mad by his beautiful love letters. She says that, at first, she loved only his beauty, but now she has forgotten about his beauty and loves his inner self, the soul she felt in the letters. When Roxane says she would love him even if he were ugly, Christian is miserable. He sends her to go speak to the cadets and to smile at them because they are about to die.

SUMMARY — ACT IV, SCENE IX

Christian tells Cyrano that Roxane is no longer in love with him. Instead, he says, she loves his "soul" and that means she loves Cyrano. He accuses Cyrano of secretly returning her love. Cyrano cannot deny it. Christian says that Cyrano must tell Roxane and ask her to choose between them. Christian calls Roxane and runs off toward the other men. Cyrano asks Roxane if she could really love Christian if he were ugly. She says that she could. Cyrano feels ecstatic and is on the cusp of revealing his secret when suddenly they hear gunfire. Le Bret cries out for Cyrano. He whispers something in Cyrano's ear, and Cyrano says that now he can never tell Roxane his feelings. A group of men comes into the camp, carrying something. Soon, we see it is Christian's body. He is dying.

SUMMARY — ACT IV, SCENE X

The men run off to fight, and Roxane collapses over Christian's body. Cyrano leans down and whispers into Christian's ear that he told Roxane the secret, and that she chose Christian. The battle breaks out all around them and Christian closes his eyes, dead. Next to Christian's heart, Roxane finds the farewell letter that Cyrano wrote for Christian to give her. She faints with grief, and Cyrano sends Ragueneau and de Guiche to take her away and protect her. Carbon emerges from the fighting, twice wounded. But the army has returned, and the men will win if they can hold out only a little longer. Cyrano tells Carbon not to worry. Now, he says, he has two deaths to avenge: Christian's and his own. Cyrano charges into battle. When he hears a Spaniard ask, "Who are these men who are so eager for death?" he begins to sing the song of the Cadets of Gascoyne. Cyrano charges off into a hail of bullets, singing as he fights.

ANALYSIS — ACT IV, SCENES VI–X

The theme of inner versus outer beauty escalates and comes to a climax during the battle scene. Even as Roxane reveals that she values inner beauty more than physical attractiveness, Cyrano has been forging letters to her. His actions call into question his own integrity and open up the possibility that ultimately, he has calculated to win Roxane himself. Cyrano's character appears tarnished at the very moment his words move Roxane to honor inner goodness. Her announcement completes the dissection and destruction of the romantic hero that Cyrano and Christian together created. Playing different halves of the hero, both Cyrano and Christian have proven to be inadequate. Because Cyrano cannot take credit for winning Roxane's love without revealing his duplicity, the play's triumphant moment belongs to love and to poetry, not to Cyrano.

The irony of this scene is staggering. Roxane travels far and takes great risks to tell Christian her wonderful news, and it turns out to be the worst news that Christian, and even Cyrano, could possibly hear. Still, Cyrano commits another act of tremendous chivalry when he consoles Christian—and tells him that Roxane picked Christian—just before he dies. Christian dies an honorable and happy death, as a good soldier and a fulfilled lover. Cyrano would rather spend the rest of his life apart from the woman he loves than dishonor the memory of his friend.

Moreover, Christian's death symbolizes the death of the superficial half of the romantic hero. By denouncing the value of outer beauty, Roxane renders Christian an unimportant and useless part of the composite romantic hero. Though she doesn't know it, Roxane loves the other half, the soul of the hero, played by Cyrano. Christian quickly dies and disappears from the play. Yet his death also prevents Cyrano from telling Roxane the truth and perhaps from making a moral mistake—dishonestly winning her love.

The war parallels the emotional war between the main characters. The climax of the play occurs on the battlefield when Christian,

Cyrano, and Roxane interact with startling dialogue and emotion. The tension between Christian and Cyrano eases, dissolving the fused romantic hero they had attempted to become.

As Cyrano's duplicity intensifies, de Guiche begins to redeem himself. He turns out to be a Gascon under all his Parisian trappings. One of the soldiers reveals that de Guiche has a Gascon accent. Because the main conflict in *Cyrano de Bergerac* lies within Cyrano, Rostand transforms his rather superficial villain into a newly minted hero without sacrificing the play's dramatic drive.

ACT V, SCENES I-VI

For fourteen years you played the part of an old friend who came to be amusing!

(See QUOTATIONS, p. 47)

SUMMARY — ACT V, SCENE, I

Fifteen years later, in 1655, the nuns of the Convent of the Ladies of the Cross in Paris talk about Cyrano. They say he makes them laugh, and they remark how he has come every week for more than ten years to visit his cousin Roxane, who first came to live in the convent after the death of her husband.

SUMMARY — ACT V, SCENE II

Roxane enters the park of the convent accompanied by de Guiche, who, now an old man, is still magnificent and one of the most powerful nobles in France. He asks Roxane if she is still faithful to Christian's memory, and she says she is. He asks if she has forgiven him, and she replies, "I am here." She says that she always wears Christian's last letter next to her heart. She tells de Guiche that Cyrano comes to visit her every week and gives her an impromptu gazette, telling her all the news. Le Bret enters and tells Roxane and de Guiche that things are going badly for Cyrano—he is old, poor, and disliked by a host of enemies as a result of his constant satirical attacks on hypocrites in society. De Guiche says that they should not pity him, because Cyrano lives his life as he chooses. De Guiche says that he would be proud to shake Cyrano's hand. Privately, de Guiche tells Le Bret that he has heard at court that some nobles are planning to kill Cyrano. Le Bret agrees to try to keep Cyrano at home.

Summary — Act V, scene iii

Ragueneau rushes in and appears upset. As Roxane leaves to talk with de Guiche, Ragueneau tells Le Bret that as Cyrano strolled beneath a high window, some lackeys pushed a massive log of wood down onto him, breaking his skull. He is barely alive. If he tries to raise his head, he may die. Le Bret and Ragueneau hasten to his side.

Summary — Act V, scene iv

After they leave, Roxane reemerges and sits down beneath an autumn tree to sew. A nun announces Cyrano's arrival.

Summary — Act V, scene v

Cyrano enters. He is pale and seems to be suffering. But he talks happily to Roxane, becoming solemn only when he tells her that he must go before nightfall. Roxane protests, then reminds Cyrano to tease the nuns, and he stuns Sister Marthe by cheerfully declaring that he will let her pray for him that night at vespers. Cyrano gives Roxane a comical summary of the news of the court, but his face becomes more and more tortured, and he finally loses consciousness.

Roxane runs to his side, and he comes to, telling her his injury meant nothing and is merely an old wound. Roxane touches her heart and says they all have their old wounds. Cyrano asks about Christian's letter and reminds Roxane that he would like to read it someday. She says it is stained with blood and tears and is therefore hard to read. But she gives it to him, and he begins to read the words he wrote for her so many years ago.

Twilight begins to fall, and Roxane sits amazed by the voice with which Cyrano reads the letter. She gradually realizes that she remembers hearing that voice under her balcony. Meanwhile, as darkness falls, she realizes that Cyrano is still able to read the letter. Suddenly, it all becomes clear to her, and she exclaims that she has realized that it was Cyrano all along. He denies it, but she now knows the truth. She asks why he kept silent for so long, since the tears on the letter belonged to him. Cyrano replies that the blood belonged to Christian.

Summary — Act V, scene vi

Suddenly, Ragueneau and Le Bret rush in and announce with horror that Cyrano has come to the convent in a physically weakened state. Cyrano says he has not finished his gazette. He adds that on Saturday the 26th, an hour before dinner, Monsieur de Bergerac was murdered. He removes his hat and shows his head swathed in bandages. He says it is ironic that he, who longed to die laughing on the sword of a hero, took his mortal blow from someone who ambushed him with a log.

Ragueneau begins to cry and, outraged, tells Cyrano that Molière has stolen a scene of Ragueneau's for his new play. Cyrano asks if the audience liked it, and Ragueneau says that they laughed and laughed. Cyrano says that his role in life has been to inspire others: Molière has genius, Christian had good looks, but he is doomed always to be hidden beneath the balcony while someone else receives the kiss. Roxane cries that Cyrano cannot die. She says she loves him. But realizing that he is dying, Roxane cries out that she loved only one man in her life, and now she has lost him—twice.

Cyrano becomes delirious. He recites a cheerful, jaunty poem about his life and subsequently falls back into a chair. Roxane breaks into sobs. Cyrano pushes himself up and says that he will not die lying down. He rises and, leaning against a tree, draws his sword. He says that he sees the skeleton of death "daring" to look at his nose. He begins to fight against invisible enemies, calling out their names: Lies, Prejudice, Cowardice, Stupidity, and Compromise.

Cyrano declares that his enemies have taken all his laurels, but that in spite of them, when he meets God that night, he will carry one thing that no one can take away from him. Suddenly, he drops his sword and falls into the arms of Le Bret and Ragueneau. Roxane kisses him on the forehead and asks what immaculate thing he will take to heaven with him. As he dies, Cyrano opens his eyes and looks at her. He replies, "My white plume."

ANALYSIS — ACT V, SCENES I-VI

Act V is the play's dramatic epilogue. Set fifteen years after the main action, the poignant tragedy of this act ties up the story line following Christian's death. The setting of this section of the play is important—it takes place at twilight on an autumn day. Both the hour and the season connote endings, changes, and death. The setting also serves as a metaphor for Roxane's changing view of physical beauty. Her realization that Cyrano wrote the letters occurs only when she notices Cyrano reading Christian's farewell letter in the dark. Once the outward visual signs lose their importance, Roxane hears Cyrano's true voice and words. The metaphorical setting creates a highly sentimental ending. Indeed, one common criticism of the play is that its final scenes become swooning and melodramatic.

Cyrano's death scene mimics his overall plight. Denied the chance to die in battle on the sword of a hero, he instead dies after being ambushed by a falling log. Cyrano's death, like his character, is simultaneously tragic, ironic, and comedic. However, he always manages to elude his fated failure, and he dies fighting not against a mortal hero but against the specters of falsehood, cowardice, and compromise—all of his "old enemies." Throughout the play, Cyrano suffers both because of his appearance and because of his unwillingness to sacrifice his principles. By this time, his long nose has become a symbol of his honorable nature and a reminder of its consequences. Cyrano dies fighting unconquerable vices but he knowing that Roxane loves him at last, despite his appearance. He says he will take his unstained white plume with him to heaven—the white plume is the mark of a leader on the battlefield and the symbol of courage. He may die, but his honor will remain pure and unstained.

Cyrano's painful realization that his life has been a failure looms over the brief bits of humor. He argues that his life has been largely unfulfilling despite moments of fleeting success. Throughout the play, Cyrano has displayed courage and bravado, but he never attains his goals or realizes his dreams. Tragically, Roxane comes to know his secret and love him only after he has been dealt his final blow. For these reasons, some critics consider *Cyrano de Bergerac* a heroic tragedy rather than a heroic comedy.

Important Quotations Explained

     VALVERT: Your nose is . . . very big.
                 CYRANO: Yes, very.
                 VALVERT: Ha!
                 CYRANO: Is that all?

This speech appears in Act I, just after Cyrano makes his first entrance. After several characters describe Cyrano to those who do not know him, Cyrano appears and fulfills everyone's expectations. Valvert, one of de Guiche's men, pokes fun at the size of Cyrano's nose—a big mistake. Cyrano makes fun of Valvert's lack of creativity and eloquence, and proceeds to put on a jesting exhibition of sorts, making fun of his own nose. This quotation demonstrates several of Cyrano's important qualities: eloquence, sense of humor, creativity, resourcefulness, courage, and confidence, as well as his showmanship and bravado. Remembering the promise he made to Roxane to keep Christian safe, Cyrano responds to Valvert's ridiculing of his nose with biting, ironic criticism instead of violence.

2.   ROXANE: His face shines with wit and intelligence.
                  He's proud, noble, young, fearless,
                  handsome. . . .
         CYRANO: Handsome!
         ROXANE: What is it? What's the matter?
         CYRANO: Nothing. . . . It's . . . it's . . . it's only a
                  twinge of pain from this little scratch.

Roxane and Cyrano's meeting in Ragueneau's shop, early in Act II,
heightens the play's drama and suspense. Roxane speaks to Cyrano
about a man she loves, who she thinks loves her. Roxane acts a bit
mysteriously, choosing to be discreet in her revelation of the man's
identity. As she reveals his identity, Cyrano thinks that she might be
referring to him—after all, each piece of information fits him. When
she says that this man is "handsome," however, Cyrano becomes
certain that she is not talking about him, and that she must be talking about someone else. Cyrano reacts by cringing and reeling in
pain. To cover up for his heartbreak, he quickly invents an excuse
for his noticeable pain: his hand wound. This moment also highlights Cyrano's weakening self-confidence and self-esteem. He now
believes that Roxane will never love him. With this idea firmly
planted in his mind, he agrees to help Christian win her love.

3.   CHRISTIAN: I need eloquence, and I have none!
      CYRANO: I'll lend you mine! Lend me your
                conquering physical charm, and
                together we'll form a romantic hero!
    Christian: What do you mean?
      Cyrano: Do you feel capable of repeating what I
                tell you every day?
    Christian: Are you suggesting . . .
      Cyrano: Roxane won't be disillusioned!
                Together, we can win her heart! Will
                you let my soul pass from my leather
                jerkin and lodge beneath your
                embroidered doublet?

Here, at the end of Act II, Cyrano and Christian talk about winning Roxane's love. Cyrano is the first of the two to realize that they can combine their powers—Cyrano's wit and poetry, Christian's good looks and charm—in an effort to woo her. Essentially, they would become one person, as Cyrano states, a "romantic hero." In a sense, both Christian and Cyrano represent stereotypes. Christian is unpoetic yet has stunning beauty, while Cyrano perfectly fills the role of the intelligent but unattractive intellectual.

One of the play's central questions is whether the combination of these traits can create a character superior to Cyrano or Christian. Indeed, initially it seems that the blending of their perfections results in nothing more than a flawless composite character. It's no surprise that Roxane falls for such a character. The only complicating factor in their scheme, however, is the duplicity required to execute their plot. Cyrano and Christian must both lie to the woman they supposedly love to win her affection. We should expect the composite romantic hero to meet his demise for sacrificing his integrity. Ultimately, however, Roxane ignores this betrayal. Upon discovering Christian and Cyrano's plan years later, she simply reinterprets her original love for Christian as love for Cyrano, saying that she has loved only one man, but lost him twice.

4.   CHRISTIAN: And now?
        ROXANE: Your true self has prevailed over your
                  outer appearance. I now love you for
                  your soul alone.
     CHRISTIAN: Oh, Roxane!
        ROXANE: . . . But you can be happy now: your
                  thoughts outshine your face. Your
                  handsomeness was what
                  first attracted me, but now that
                  my eyes are open I no longer see it!

This quotation, which comes in Act IV just after Roxane arrives at
Arras and surprises the cadets, heightens the sense of tension in the
play. Roxane's changing sentiments have derailed Christian and
Cyrano's plan. Just before Christian is about to go off to battle,
Roxane tells him that he loves him for his "soul alone" and no
longer for his "outer appearance." This seemingly positive romantic
development troubles and depresses Christian since he essentially
borrowed his "soul" from Cyrano—without his outer appearance,
he has nothing to offer Roxane. Roxane rejects the romantic hero's
mixture of inner and outer beauty in favor of the poetry and inner
beauty that she initially attributes to Christian. Christian, however,
understands that he had nothing to do with the poetry, and that
Roxane really loves Cyrano without even knowing it. The moment
is ironic since what Roxane believes to be her statement of true, lasting love for Christian is based upon a character trait that Christian
does not possess.

QUOTATIONS

5.   ROXANE: . . . . How can you read now? It's dark.
                          And for fourteen years you played the
                          part of an old friend who came to
                          be amusing!
    CYRANO: Roxane!
    ROXANE: It was you.
    CYRANO: No, Roxane, no!

In the fifth and final act, Roxane begins to realize that Cyrano wrote all the letters and spoke outside her window on Christian's behalf. As dusk settles, Cyrano begins to read Christian's last letter out loud. Roxane is amazed at his ability to read so well in the read. Cyrano is reciting the letter from memory. Seeing tears roll down his face, she conjectures that the tears on the letter were his all along. Cyrano says that the blood was Christian's. Cyrano's declaration is symbolic because his tears and Christian's blood have combined on the letter. Together they represent the collaboration that formed the man—the "romantic hero"—that Roxane loves.

    When Roxane accuses him of writing and speaking on Christian's behalf, Cyrano firmly denies it. Roxane refuses to believe him and laments that she has loved only one man, and lost him twice.

KEY FACTS

FULL TITLE
Cyrano de Bergerac: Heroic Comedy in Five Acts

AUTHOR
Edmond Rostand

TYPE OF WORK
Play

GENRE
Heroic comedy, verse play

LANGUAGE
French

TIME AND PLACE WRITTEN
Paris, France, 1897

DATE OF FIRST PERFORMANCE
December 28, 1897

DATE OF FIRST PUBLICATION
1898

PUBLISHER
Charpentier et Fasquelle

TONE
Grandiose, heroic

SETTING (TIME)
1640 (Acts I–IV) and 1655 (Act V)

SETTING (PLACE)
Paris and Arras

PROTAGONIST
Cyrano de Bergerac

MAJOR CONFLICT
Cyrano loves Roxane but feels he is too ugly to woo her; Cyrano must overcome the severe self-doubt and shame that result from his awkward appearance in order to reveal to Roxane that he wrote Christian's love letters.

KEY FACTS

RISING ACTION

Roxane asks Cyrano to protect Christian, who is fighting in a war alongside Cyrano, and Cyrano agrees to help Christian court Roxane by writing love letters and allowing Christian to sign them.

CLIMAX

Roxane tells Christian she loves him for his soul and not for his physical appearance. Just before Christian dies, Cyrano lies by telling him that Roxane has learned of the forged letters and has chosen Christian over Cyrano. Simultaneously, he recognizes that he can never tell Roxane that he is the true author of Christian's love letters.

FALLING ACTION

Cyrano visits Roxane and learns of his role in helping Christian. She declares her love for him, but Cyrano, who has been mortally wounded before visiting Roxane, dies.

THEMES

Values and virtue; inner and outer beauty; the danger in deception

MOTIFS

Society; the letters; fighting and war

SYMBOLS

Individual characters; Cyrano's nose; Cyrano's tears and Christian's blood

FORESHADOWING

Cyrano tries to write a letter to Roxane before they meet.

Study Questions & Essay Topics

Study Questions

1. *Compare and contrast Cyrano and Christian. Do they have any similarities besides their love for Roxane? Why is Cyrano so sad when Christian dies, apart from his realization that he himself will never be able to tell Roxane he loves her? Is there any other reason?*

Cyrano and Christian are mutual foils and virtual opposites in their attributes: Cyrano is brilliant and looks ridiculous; Christian is simple but beautiful. Cyrano is interested in love and hopes to use Roxane to help attain it, whereas Christian is interested in Roxane and hopes to use love to attain her. But they are both courageous, noble individuals—Christian's grief when Roxane admits she would love him even if he were ugly indicates his honorable, if only partially realized, recognition of his complicity and guilt. Cyrano's grief over Christian's death is due as much to the loss of a good friend and a good soul as it is to the end of his romantic hopes for Roxane, not to mention his hopes for romance in general.

2.   *How does the play's comedic style change in Act III? Why do you think Rostand changes his tactics at this point? After Act III, is it still fair to call the play a comedy?*

In the first two acts, the comedy of the play centers around the bombast of Cyrano's character; the source of the humor lies mainly in the surprise and wonderment that a person could look and behave as Cyrano does, particularly when directing his scorching wit at less intelligent characters. In Act III, the play adopts a much more sophisticated, complicated dramatic irony to achieve its humorous effects, and Rostand occasionally uses the conceit of parody, specifically parodying the balcony scene from *Romeo and Juliet*. Rostand probably realized that once we familiarize ourselves with Cyrano, we need new sources of humor to maintain interest. The last two acts, with the starving troops and the deaths of Christian and Cyrano, lack the same comic tone and development present in the first three. They still have humor—Cyrano taunting de Guiche and teasing the nuns, for instance—but the mood of the acts is far more serious, as is the treatment of character.

3. *Is Roxane worthy of the love that Cyrano feels for her, or
    is she simply a romantic ideal of womanhood to him?*

Roxane's attributes demonstrate that she is worthy of Cyrano's love
in several ways. Of all the women in the play, Roxane is the *most*
beautiful, intelligent, and graceful. As the play develops, she proves
herself intrepid (driving her coach through the Spanish army), brave
(remaining with the troops during the battle), and loyal (staying
faithful to Christian's memory for fifteen years after his death). Le
Bret realizes at once that Roxane is the only woman Cyrano could
possibly love. But the flatness with which Rostand portrays Roxane
suggests that we have too little information to evaluate her character definitively. We know very little about her, and several of the
things we do know could be sources of criticism: her friends are pre-
tentious and her methods are sometimes devious (she manipulates
the Capuchin into marrying her to Christian). Moreover, most of
what we learn about her involves male characters rhapsodizing on
the way that they feel in her presence. Perhaps Rostand's flat portrayal of Roxane highlights the shallowness of Cyrano's and Christian's affections.

QUESTIONS & ESSAYS

SUGGESTED ESSAY TOPICS

1. What values does Cyrano live by? How does he put his values into practice? How does his ridiculous nose affect his life?

2. What makes *Cyrano de Bergerac* a historical romance rather than a realistic evocation of a time and place? What are some of the ways in which Rostand works *The Three Musketeers* into his story line?

3. Discuss the development of de Guiche from a scheming politician into a valiant Gascon soldier. What enables him to accomplish his transformation? Does he sustain it until the end of the play?

4. Does *Cyrano de Bergerac* have a happy ending? Why or why not?

5. What would Cyrano's life be like if he did not have such an outstanding nose? Would he have the same personality, feelings, or outlook on the world? Discuss.

Review & Resources

Quiz

1. What does Cyrano say he will take with him to heaven?

    A. His sword
    B. His white plume
    C. His nose
    D. One of Ragueneau's pastries

2. Who hires the hundred men to kill Ligniere?

    A. Comte de Guiche
    B. Cardinal Richelieu
    C. Cyrano
    D. Valvert

3. Why is Roxane worried for Christian's safety among the Cadets of Gascoyne?

    A. He is not a skilled fighter
    B. He has written a scathing satire about the cadets
    C. He is hot-tempered and tends to pick fights
    D. The Cadets of Gascoyne tend to pick on anyone who is not a Gascon

4. Whom does de Guiche propose as possible patrons for Cyrano in Act II?

    A. Richelieu and Valvert
    B. Valvert and himself
    C. Richelieu and himself
    D. He says that Cyrano does not need a patron

5. Where are Roxane and Christian married?

   A. On the battlefield
   B. In Roxane's house
   C. In the convent
   D. At the Chapel of St. Beatrice

6. Who tells Christian about the plot to kill Ligniere?

   A. A pickpocket
   B. Cyrano
   C. Ragueneau
   D. De Guiche

7. What is Cyrano's relation to Roxane?

   A. He is her uncle
   B. He is her brother-in-law
   C. He is her cousin
   D. He is not related to her; he hopes to become her husband

8. What does de Guiche do with the white plume after Cyrano produces it?

   A. He waves it as a signal to a spy
   B. He tucks it into his pocket angrily
   C. He tears it to shreds
   D. He throws it to the ground

9. How does Christian prove his bravery to the cadets?

   A. He challenges Valvert to a duel
   B. He proclaims his love for Roxane
   C. He insults Cyrano's nose
   D. He steals Carbon's sword

10. Why does Christian's action go unpunished?

   A. Valvert is a terrible swordsman
   B. Roxane thinks he means someone else
   C. Cyrano has promised Roxane to protect Christian
   D. Carbon steals the sword back without saying a word

REVIEW & RESOURCES

11. Why are the cadets hungry at the siege of Arras?

    A. They are besieged and their supply lines have been cut by the Spanish army

    B. De Guiche did not order enough rations before the company left France

    C. The peasants have burned their crops, making foraging impossible

    D. To prove their valor, the cadets refuse to eat before battle

12. How does Cyrano distract de Guiche while Roxane and Christian are being married?

    A. By pretending to be a Spanish spy

    B. By pretending to have fallen from the moon

    C. By pretending to be Valvert

    D. By challenging him to a duel

13. How does Cyrano win a pair of minstrels for a day?

    A. By defeating the king's best musketeer in a duel

    B. By correctly guessing the note they were playing

    C. By defeating Valvert in a horse race

    D. By winning a bet over a question of grammar

14. Why does Cyrano hate Montfleury?

    A. Because he is hideously fat

    B. Because he once mocked Cyrano's nose

    C. Because he dared to smile at Roxane

    D. Because he refuses to act in Cyrano's play

15. How does Cyrano treat the nuns in Roxane's convent?

    A. He teases them fondly

    B. He is solemn and respectful

    C. He ignores them because they do not concern him

    D. He hates their Christian hypocrisy

16. How does Roxane discover that Cyrano wrote the letters?

    A. Christian tells her
    B. Cyrano tells her
    C. Through a keyhole, she spies Cyrano writing her
    D. She observes that he is able to read one of the letters aloud even in the dark

17. How is Cyrano dealt his mortal wound?

    A. In battle against the Spanish
    B. A giant log is dropped on him from a high window
    C. In a duel against de Guiche
    D. In a duel against Christian

18. Why does Ragueneau's marriage fail?

    A. He falls in love with the duenna
    B. He and his wife argue over the children's futures
    C. His wife leaves him for a musketeer
    D. His wife leaves him for a poor poet

19. Where does Cyrano meet Roxane in Act II?

    A. In Ragueneau's bakery
    B. In the park at the convent
    C. In the orchard at her house
    D. In the kitchen of the palace

20. How often does Cyrano write Roxane on Christian's behalf during the siege of Arras?

    A. Monthly
    B. Weekly
    C. Daily
    D. Hourly

21. Who insults Cyrano's nose most often during the play?

    A. Christian
    B. Valvert
    C. De Guiche
    D. Cyrano

REVIEW & RESOURCES

22. How does Christian die?

    A. Cyrano kills him over Roxane
    B. De Guiche kills him over Roxane
    C. Valvert kills him over Roxane
    D. He dies in battle at the siege of Arras

23. Why doesn't Cyrano buy himself dinner after the duel in the theater?

    A. He is not hungry
    B. He prefers to wait until he has defeated the hundred men
    C. He tossed all his money to Bellerose
    D. He tossed all his money to Le Bret

24. Who kills de Guiche?

    A. Cyrano
    B. Christian
    C. Valvert
    D. De Guiche lives to the end of the play

25. *Cyrano de Bergerac* takes place during which two years?

    A. 1789 and 1805
    B. 1500 and 1550
    C. 1640 and 1655
    D. 1830 and 1845

Answer Key:
1: B; 2: A; 3: D; 4: C; 5: B; 6: A; 7: C; 8: A; 9: C; 10: C; 11: A; 12: B; 13: D; 14: C; 15: A; 16: D; 17: B; 18: C; 19: A; 20: C; 21: D; 22: D; 23: C; 24: D; 25: C

SUGGESTIONS FOR FURTHER READING

FREEMAN, EDWARD. *Edmond Rostand, Cyrano de Bergerac.* Glasgow, Scotland: University of Glasgow French and German Publications, 1995.

GRANT, ELLIOTT MANSFIELD, ed. *Chief French Plays of the Nineteenth Century.* New York: Harper & Brothers, 1934.

HARTH, ERICA. CYRANO DE BERGERAC *and the Polemics of Modernity.* New York: Columbia University Press, 1970.

——*Ideology and Culture in Seventeenth-Century France.* Ithaca: Cornell University Press, 1983.

HUGHES, HENRY. *Afterword of Cyrano de Bergerac: Heroic Comedy in Five Acts.* Translated by Lowell Bair. New York: Signet Classic, 1972.

LANIUS, EDWARD W. *Cyrano de Bergerac and the Universe of the Imagination.* Geneva: Broz, 1967.

RYLAND, HOBART. *The Sources of the Play Cyrano de Bergerac.* New York: Institute of French Studies, 1936.

WOOLLEN, GEOFF. *Introduction of Cyrano de Bergerac.* London: Bristol Classical Press, 1994.

A Note on the Type

The typeface used in SparkNotes study guides is Sabon, created by master typographer Jan Tschichold in 1964. Tschichold revolutionized the field of graphic design twice: first with his use of asymmetrical layouts and sanserif type in the 1930s when he was affiliated with the Bauhaus, then by abandoning assymetry and calling for a return to the classic ideals of design. Sabon, his only extant typeface, is emblematic of his latter program: Tschichold's design is a recreation of the types made by Claude Garamond, the great French typographer of the Renaissance, and his contemporary Robert Granjon. Fittingly, it is named for Garamond's apprentice, Jacques Sabon.